For the Love
of the
Game

by Claire Daniel
illustrated by Gina Capaldi

SCHOOL PUBLISHERS

D1798503

Printed in China

ISBN 10:   0-15-377377-4
ISBN 13:   978-0-15-377377-8

Ordering Options
ISBN 10:   0-15-377149-6 (Grade 5 Collection)
ISBN 13:   978-0-15-377149-1 (Grade 5 Collection)
ISBN 10:   0-15-377859-8 (package of 5)
ISBN 13:   978-0-15-377859-9 (package of 5)

2 3 4 5 6 7 8 9 10   0940   17 16 15 14 13 12 11 10 09

Spring is a great time of year. It is when baseball season begins, and baseball is my favorite sport. Spring is also a really good time of year to make some money doing chores for people.

This year, it didn't take long to get my first job. The Smiths asked me to clean their garage. It took three Saturdays, but in the end, I had enough money to buy new baseball cleats. My mom took me to get them. I knew they would help me be a better player.

Now I was working on saving up for a new baseball glove. My neighbors always had work for me. There were garages to clean, lawns to mow, dogs to walk.

Sometimes work got in the way of other things. On the first day of baseball practice, Mrs. Horton had a job for me washing her dog.

"Wash Samson," she said. "Use the towels in the garage. They are designated for the dog."

I washed Samson, knowing that I would be in trouble with the coach. However, I began to feel better when I thought of the money I would make.

Finally, Samson was dry, and I was a little richer. I arrived at the baseball field. I apologized to Coach Burundi for being late, and he merely said, "What position do you plan on playing?"

"Shortstop," I said. In my opinion, that was the best position to play.

"Field some balls," he said, guiding me over to the outfield where some players were catching balls. "Don't show up late again," he said.

"Yes, sir!" I replied, and I was determined to keep my word.

We practiced for another hour, and I got to know my new teammates. Now, I don't want to sound conceited, but I have always been a good player. Some might even call me a baseball maven, perfect for the position of shortstop.

The second day of practice, I showed up seconds before starting time. The coach glanced at his watch to check the time. I tried to get there earlier, but Mrs. Lee's dog had been in slow motion on our walk. My dad had to race over to practice to drop me off.

At the end of practice, the coach held an extra batting session. I couldn't stay because I had to walk Mr. Laurel's dog. I told myself it didn't matter. I was getting closer to buying the glove that would make me a better player.

Every day that week, I had to cut baseball practice short. I had work. I didn't mind missing a little practice. Last year, I was the best hitter on the team, and besides, I was thinking about that glove. I had my eye on a brand new bat, too.

Saturday's practice was scheduled for three o'clock in the afternoon, so I had plenty of time to do my homework and chores around the house. It also gave me enough time to do one small job for Mrs. Horton. I arrived at her house at around one o'clock to clean her car. This turned out to be an easy task, and it added to my savings.

As soon as I finished, Mrs. Horton said, "Arnie, I have one more thing." She led me outside and pointed to two wooden lawn chairs. "I'll pay you twenty dollars to paint both chairs," she said.

I felt exhilarated. That would give me enough money for the glove! Then I remembered baseball practice.

"I don't think I can, Mrs. Horton," I said. "I have baseball practice. Can I do it tomorrow?"

"Oh, I'm afraid I need the chairs painted right away. I am going to use them for my garden party tomorrow," she said. "I'll just have to do it myself."

I thought for a moment. I would do it. I would just have to work fast.

Of course, everything went wrong. The paintbrush was so small that it took forever to paint the chairs. The wood was so dry that it needed two coats. By the time I finished, I was already late for practice.

When I finally arrived at the field, it was four o'clock, and everyone was sitting in the bleachers. The coach had a smirk on his face. I looked away.

Coach Burundi was saying, "I think we have what it takes to win a lot of games this year! For five years straight, the Wildcats have reigned as champs. This year, we're going to give them a run for their money!"

Then his talk turned into a pep rally. He yelled, "Now, what do we say?"

"Tigers can't be beat!" the team replied.

Then I noticed that all the kids were heading out to do final drills. Suddenly, I felt mortified. I had missed the entire practice.

Coach Burundi was writing notes. I cleared my throat.

"I'm sorry I'm so late," I said.

He said, "You're sitting on the bench for the first game. That is, if you can manage to come on time. If you don't, then you are off the team. . .for good."

"Coach," I protested, "I tried."

"Arnie, listen to me," he said, sitting down next to me on the bleachers. "Last year, you were a great shortstop. You hit the ball well, and you were a good team player. This year is different. Your mind isn't on the game. If you come to practice at all, you come late. You pop out more than you get on base. You are not as quick on your feet as you used to be. Your teammates are getting better because they practice and work hard."

I didn't say anything. I couldn't argue. He was right— about everything.

He added, "You need practice, and you're not getting it because you're not here enough."

He got up, and said, "Do you love the game?"

"Of course," I said.

He said, "Well, if you really do, and you want to play shortstop, then you're going to have to work harder."

I walked home tossing the ball from hand to hand. Then I looked at my glove and realized for the first time that it was fine. What was I doing? I was giving up the game I loved for a new glove, when the glove I had now was fine. At this rate, I might get the new glove but not have a chance to use it.

Coach Burundi kept his word. I sat on the bench for most of the first game. As I watched everybody play, I realized how much better they had become. I thought about the money I had saved, but if I couldn't play baseball, it meant nothing.

Fortunately, my story had a happy ending. I did go ahead and buy the glove, but that was not all. More importantly, I was never late for practice again, and Coach Burundi rewarded me by letting me play second base. It wasn't shortstop, but it was an important position.

Coach Burundi gave me some batting tips, and he suggested that I open up my legs a little bit when I stood at homeplate. I was playing baseball again and loving it.

My neighbors still called and asked me to do odd jobs, and sometimes I went to help. Now there was only one difference. Sometimes, I said no—especially during baseball season.

Think Critically

1. Why was Arnie put on the bench?

2. How did Arnie's feelings about money change from the beginning to the end of the story?

3. Why do you think Arnie's coach didn't kick him off the team right away?

4. What was the problem in the story and how was it resolved?

5. What did you learn from the story?

 **Health**

Exercise Warm-Up Use the Internet or reference books to find information on why you should warm-up before you exercise. Make a list of some warm-up exercises.

School-Home Connection Prepare a list of five or more questions to ask family members or friends about a sport they have played. Ask questions such as how they learned to play the game and why they like the game.

Word Count: 1,229